# STRATEGIES

## TO MAKE SURE YOUR BUSINESS THRIVES DURING THE NEXT CRISIS

by
Horatiu Sasu

**_Disclaimer_**

All material contained in this eBook is provided for educational, guide and informational purposes ONLY. No responsibility can be taken for any results or outcomes resulting from the use of this eBook. The directions described within this eBook are the author's personal thoughts and are not intended to be a definitive set of procedures. You may discover that there are other methods and materials to accomplish the same end result.

# INTRODUCTION

Benjamin Franklin, the great American statesman, said that there are two things we cannot avoid in this life: death and taxes. In the 21st century, we can add crises to this list. I still think that it's easier to avoid taxes, but crises are inevitable. Are you prepared? A new financial and economic crisis approaches.

Today, we don't talk about "if." We talk about "when" next crisis strikes. Several well-known economists say that the next crisis will take place very soon. This idea links with the notion that we have a crisis about every ten years, which is why they're viewing the next one as occurring from 2020 to 2021. There's basically a general consensus that a new financial and economic crisis will strike. However, there's less of a consensus about the specific causes of the future crisis.

During 20 years of consultancy, I've worked with numerous companies—small and large, public and private. Even in normal times, many of them do not know:

- How to make their business more efficient
- How to make their business a winner
- What to do to develop the business
- Which performance indicators tell them that they are on their way to success

After crafting these techniques during normal times, I realized that some of them also apply during times of crises. However, they don't all apply during crises, so you have to know the difference. For example, diversification is desirable in normal times, but it leads to bankruptcy during times of crisis. Isn't that scary?

It is scary if you don't have a plan. Creating a plan when the crisis has already hit is like building a shelter when the storm has already begun. In fact, the wise businessperson prepares his sled during summer and his boat during the winter.

So the wise businessperson is preparing for a crisis **now**, despite the season. If you do that, you only have the simple task of preserving the successful solutions you have **already** tested, so you know they'll work. Just continue developing strategies, procedures, and techniques now, before a crisis occurs. Remember, even though it may seem calm now, you'll need a contingency plan in order to thrive during crises.

It's good to make a plan, even for things you can't control and that are related to blind hazards. And out of everything we're going to discuss, it's good to do a Plan B, or even a Plan C. Why? You know very well: even in normal times, things don't always go the way we planned; even more, this situation happens in times that we're just trying to see what to expect.

Or if you prefer, we can see what to expect from history of crises: it demonstrates that 60-65% of businesses might fail **during the next crisis**, and many people will go bankrupt. Doesn't that sound horrifying?

On the other hand, some people will save their business and even thrive. Why? If they know how to lead their business through the troubled waves and along the sharp cliffs of the crisis, they will find their way to a safe haven, and experience much greater prosperity than they had before it started. This provides a fantastic opportunity for you to be among the 35-40% of businesses who will win. Then you can take the customers from the businesses who fail. Tell me: which category will the criers be in—the 65% or the 35%?

When you change your viewpoint from threat to opportunity, something miraculous happens: blockages disappear, and opportunities appear out of nowhere. People emerge from the unknown, and there are favorable occasions, even in the changes that others think are spiteful. And in a short amount of time, a crisis becomes your ally, not your enemy.

Well, wouldn't it be great if there was never another crisis? Yeah, it would!

Now I remember a joke: a man who wasn't feeling very well went to his doctor.

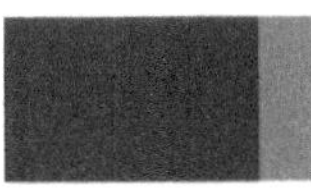



The doctor said, "I have good news and bad news. Which do you want me to start with?"

The patient replied, "The bad news."

"Your lungs are only half of their average dimensions."

"So what's the good news?"

"Well," the doctor said, "Your liver has enough room to grow."

It's a joke, but a crisis means that there's a problem with the system, and we have plenty of problems in our system. If you understand the signs, you have the chance to take measures that will save you. So do you understand the signs, or live in denial? You're like a patient who denies the results of an X-ray. If he recognizes the signs, he needs to see a doctor.

Don't try to guess when a crisis will occur. See if there's already a crisis in your backyard, and find out what you have to do to prepare for it.

Start with this basic question: How does a firm work? Many of the businesses are products of their environment. If the economy grows, many businesses also grow. Is the economy failing? Then a lot of business fail, too!

But a business must grow, regardless of the circumstances that surround them.

How to do it?

There are lots of theories. But there's no way to practice solutions during a crisis!

Here's another problem you must solve before the next crisis: economic experts do not always agree with one other, not even in times of economic stability. I think you've noticed how these experts contradict each other. What's true and "proven" for some of them is torn down by others.

Remember, experts do not always agree with each other, even during times of economic stability. European managerial strategies are contested in the United States. Measurement tools that succeed in China may not work in Egypt.

Start with this basic question: How does a firm work? Many of the businesses are products of their environment. If the economy grows, many businesses also grow. Is the economy failing? Then a lot of business fail, too!

But a business must grow, regardless of the circumstances that surround them.

How to do it?

There are lots of theories. But there's no way to practice solutions during a crisis!

Here's another problem you must solve before the next crisis: economic experts do not always agree with one other, not even in times of economic stability. I think you've noticed how these experts contradict each other. What's true and "proven" for some of them is torn down by others.

Remember, experts do not always agree with each other, even during times of economic stability. European managerial strategies are contested in the United States. Measurement tools that succeed in China may not work in Egypt.

But here's the good news:

I'll provide you with options. You don't need to pay consultants and experts small fortunes, in order to effectively prepare for a crisis. No, you can apply these methods yourself. But only implement them one at a time, not all at once. Remember, this practice requires patience and an open mind.

**So let's start with the most important must-do...**

# 1 Avoid the Ostrich Maneuver!

Many people are afraid to actively seek out solutions for preparing for crises. They prefer the ostrich policy: has somebody announced that the future will be horrible? We deny it! And if we deny it, it will not exist. Wow, we solved the problem!

These kinds of people refuse to look ahead for solutions, hoping that... *what*? I was tempted to deny facts that show that the whole world would only need one little kick for the present system to disintegrate into painful noise. I was tempted to deny facts. If you feel like you're tempted to do the same, ask yourself: *"What am I trying to deny? What am I trying to avoid? If I remain in denial, does that mean it's not going to happen? If I say that this cannot happen to me, but only to others, can this attitude improve the situation?"*

Why don't we get ready now, while there's still time to do it? Why not take advantage of the calm before the storm, so we can make the most of strategies that will sustain us during crises?

A few years ago, when the 2008 crisis was about to ease up, many entrepreneurs and managers believed that it was only a matter of time before a new crisis occurred. The crisis didn't happen when they expected it, but this information is concerning: in a survey, only 50% of managers or entrepreneurs said they had a contingency plan, and only a quarter said that this plan would be effective.

They knew very well what a crisis would bring:

- All the chaos in their company's operations and procedures
- All the disruptions in their relationships with suppliers and customers
- All the undelivered goods and missed payments
- The danger that the Sword of Damocles would permanently close the business.

Yet only a quarter of them had an effective strategy for a future crisis. Are you among the **25%** who have a relatively effective plan, or the **75%** who have no plan?

Which boat do you want to stay in? The one that's properly prepared and thrives, or the one that ignores an impending crisis and complains about it?

But how should we prepare? To find out my advice, carefully read the following information:

**Let's prepare for the worst, and be happy if it's not as bad as we imagined. Let's make a plan that includes anything we can't control in our business.**

But always make sure that you...

# 2 Find out how other people succeeded during the former crisis

There are financial and economic crises everywhere. However, a lot of businesspeople thrived in the crisis. This success started with the stubbornness of some entrepreneurs, who saw an opportunity during a crisis. That's exactly what we'll see. Yes, the foundations of many honest fortunes are laid during crises!

Let me tell you a story: at the low point of the Great Depression (1929-1930), when everybody was desperate, a family prepared a meal for hungry workers that arrived at their oil station. The food was so good that more and more people kept coming. They moved into a restaurant, tried to find better and more successful recipes, and succeeded during the crisis. Do you know the name? Sanders. As in Colonel Sanders.

Yes, KFC started when 60-65% of the business failed! What do you say about that?

In my searches for solutions to prepare for crises, I found the example of a restaurant that created a menu called 'The Recession Special.' It offered break-even pricing, just to get people in the door during the recession. This tactic allowed the steakhouse to remain fully staffed, and also provided the restaurant a chance to **upsell** its customers by offering them beverages while they were eating their once-in-a-lifetime-priced steak dinners. You can read more about this brilliant idea here: http://capitalistcreations.com/7-ways-to-prepare-your-business-for-the-coming-recession/.

Now, the question is: What prevents you from preparing your own Recession Special now?

Let me tell you about the worst inflation in history, in Zimbabwe.

According to globalfinancialdata.com: “In 2001, the inflation rate exceeded 100%, and in 2003, it was almost 600%. At that point, hyperinflation kicked in. Inflation rose to 1,281% in 2006, and 66,000% in 2007. In 2008, inflation hit an annualized 80 billion trillion percent (89,700,000,000,000,000,000,000) toward the end of 2008. At that point, Zimbabwe dollars were about as valuable as toilet paper.”

Other problems occurred in Zimbabwe that we might experience **during the next crisis**. The amount of money that people could withdraw from ATMs was hilarious. And when the ATMs were set to release a maximum limit of $100 billion a day, you could use that money to buy... some pencils.

But that seemed to be unimportant for some local business people. What matters is that, during an 80 billion trillion percent, businesses survived, and even thrived!

If you are interested, we can discuss a lot of examples about people that thrived during crises. Tell me if you are interested. I am passionate about these kinds of stories!

## I'm also passionate about this must-do...

# Choose 2 or 3 fields to develop in your business, in order to thrive during the next crisis

We've seen that people have found growth opportunities (or at the very least, survival opportunities) in any crisis. So let's now see **which businesses** are more likely to survive the next crisis. If the crisis is going to be harsher, I think some of them will stand out.

Here's a hint: there are many sites providing information about how **individuals** and **families** should prepare for the crisis. Some say that this information is not helpful, but I think it is crucial for finding opportunities for your business! Why? Just as Paco Lopez said, “In times of crisis, there are two kinds of people: the ones who cry, and the ones who sell handkerchiefs to those who cry!”

I think there are some fields where you can **ALREADY** start to grow a business that's destined for success in times of financial collapse. However, you can also start a business that transcends the collapse by meeting a strong need during the collapse.

There is always going to be a need for someone to fix a broken water pipe.

Generally, crises show that **small and medium-sized businesses and freelancers are more adaptable during times of crisis**—because they provide better quality, move faster, know how to negotiate prices, and are self-motivated.

Concerning the domains, I think the main industries that will withstand the crisis are:

- Food
- Goods of immediate necessity
- Any activity related to self-defense, including the defense of your family and fortune
- Anything that can help people and businesses survive during a full crisis
- Bartering

Yes, you led that last item correctly. If we experiment hyperinflation, what do you think will happen to banks when the economy crashes? What do you think will happen to YOUR money in the bank, and the money in your business' bank account? If there's any value left to money, gaining access to it will become increasingly difficult. Then what do you do? You barter: you give me a kilogram of wheat in exchange for a blouse. That's how we can manage without money!

Many people have bartered during times of crisis, and they will do it in the upcoming crisis as well. According to statistics from the International Reciprocity Trade Association, over 400,000 companies traded in barter goods for over $10 billion in the 2008 crisis.[1]

And now, an important question: **who do you think will gain fortunes then?** Of course! The one who organizes a barter faire.

In fact, I studied 15 business opportunities **during the next crisis**, including:

- **Price-comparing sites** (that will save people's money with one click)
- **Renewable energy** (if classic energy becomes more and more expensive)
- **Ye old fix-it shop** (from shoes to mechanic's shops)

---

1 http://www.time.com/time/magazine/article/0,9171,1931665,00.html?xid=rss-topstories, nov 2009

And there are a lot of them. Now we have many opportunities to hope, be it in our own business, or as associates or investors in an existing business. I'm sure **you** thought of some domains, haven't you?

Of course, you need to start developing these fields NOW, in a business that is specifically geared for financial collapse. Start from anywhere—in any field that makes your heart sing. But START! For instance, open a store, or partner with someone in the fields above or in fields that bring opportunities in YOUR region. And once things get rolling, see what direction the market takes you, and adapt! It is difficult to change tires while driving, so don't wait until the crisis starts!

Remember, write me at hello@horatiu.biz, and tell me your opinion. What fields do you think will survive in a crisis?

**What fields have you chosen to develop in your business, in order to thrive during the next crisis?**

While listing them, it's important to remember your history…

# Learn helpful teachings from the history of crises

A short history of economic crises brings us good news: in any crisis, opportunities are created to help some people thrive. Many businesses began during full crises, and developed afterward. The entire history shows that if you have the ability to modify your viewpoint, and consider change to be positive (rather than a threat), all sorts of possibilities will begin to appear.

For example, we can draw many useful lessons from the first crisis in Zimbabwe. Here are some tips from people who LIVED through the crisis:

Samuel Gumbe from the University of Zimbabwe Nyasha Kaseke University gave us veritable recommendations about manufacturing in a hyperinflationary environment.

A very useful synthesis of this teachings is here: http://www.time.com/time/magazine/article/0,9171,1931665,00.html?xid=rss-topstories, nov 2009

I learned from these very helpful teachings:

- Decentralized decision-making is important for taking care of sudden changes in an environment.
- If an organization is going to survive the effects of hyperinflation, it needs to innovate its workforce.
- Marketing is imperative for ensuring survival in a hyperinflationary environment.
- In this environment, strategic procurement is a prerequisite.
- The finance department must spearhead the preservation of wealth.

Regarding the History of Crises, what can all of these crises teach us?

- They show that life—including the life of a business—moves forward.
- Many have lost their savings, jobs, families, or homes. But life goes on, with or without us.
- The business experience of the crisis is extremely useful, in order to prepare ourselves for what awaits us.
- *A lot of businesspeople have thrived during crises.*

For example, a husband and wife earned a living by selling five-cent cakes out of their car. That's how they survived the crisis that destroyed other businesses. Right after the crisis, they sold pastries throughout Chattanooga, Tennessee. Their business developed, and became what we now know as Little Debbie Snack Cakes, which was worth 1.4 billion at the time of the recording this lesson.

Also in the countries that are having crises **today**, hundreds and thousands of entrepreneurs are thriving. They thrive through a lot of work and legal means, and they find solutions. Here's a success story from Nigeria, one of the countries affected by frequent and deep crises:
http://www.cipe.org/blog/2016/02/25/surviving-in-economic-crisis-a-nigerian-woman-entrepreneurs-story/

Also on the African continent, in times of hyperinflation, entrepreneurs have the courage to go over day-to-day challenges—including overcoming difficulty with sourcing raw materials, navigating an energy crisis, finding a skilled workforce, limiting access to funding, and understanding a lack of adequate data (from consumer behaviour to aid planning).

“Production can be challenging especially when trying to attain certain volumes with a consistent level of quality,” one entrepreneur says. But she adds: “We find creative ways to solve power issues, work with what is readily available to us in terms of raw material sourcing, and constantly train staff to develop innovative responses to external setbacks”.

See the whole story here:
http://africanbusinessmagazine.com/sectors/technology/ghanas-entrepreneurs-adapt-to-survive/

Yes, the history of crises is full of teachings that help us prepare our businesses—not only to survive, but to thrive!

Do you have **your** business plan to survive, even thrive, during the next crisis? If you don't (or if you have doubts about your current plan), let me help you start a good plan. Write me at **hello@horatiu.biz**, and tell me what's keeping you from completing the plan that will make your soul sing!

After you email me, you can learn how to...

# 5 Quickly measure and improve your performance

To succeed during a crisis, another key is knowing the key factors of success in your business—more accurately, the key performance criteria. A lot of my clients don't know what to answer when I ask them the level of income and expenditure, and how these expenses are broken down into fixed and variable costs. Very quickly, they tell me what their incomes are, but the structure of the expenses escapes them. And when we start doing the calculations together, they remain amazed.

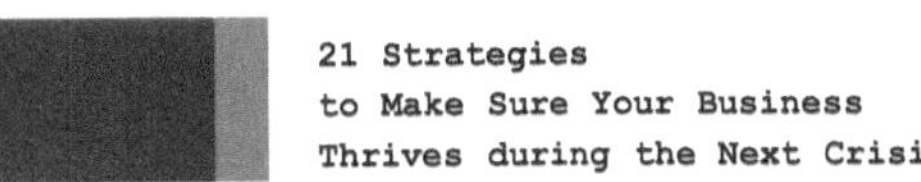



For instance, I asked a client of mine about the net-profit margin of each of his products, so that he could find out how much of a discount he could give. I asked another client of mine to tell me why he believed that even though he had income, his profit margin was very small.

However, these are just basic examples. There are certain key performance factors in each field. For example, in the case of the transportation company, the key performance criteria that will ensure success in the coming crisis include:

- A fleet adapted to customer requirements
- Economic machines optimized, both for targeted clients and businesses.
- Optimization of transport routes, given the load and the frequency of the shipment.
- The observance of the delivery terms, or even the shortening of them, at a lower price.

**What are the key factors for your company?**

Well, if you haven't asked yourself that, I suggest you research and optimize them NOW, because they will ensure your success **during the next crisis**.

**Please answer the following questions:**

- What are the key factors for your business' success? You can find them through a fast search on the internet, by reviewing interviews given by your competitors, and especially by asking your customers
- Where are you regarding these key factors, in comparsion to your competition?
- Considering that these key factors will ensure your success during a crisis, what quick measures (because there isn't much time) are you going to take to improve the company's performance?

**You check out online reviews before you go to a new restaurant, right? You can apply that same concept to the next crisis...**

# Rank yourself by comparing your business to your competition

Very simply, you can find out where you are in relation to your competitors by using a tool like the one below. In it, you can put the factors you've determined above.

For example (absolutely random viewing):

*What are the key factors of the success of your business?*

Let's say you've established (on a fast search on the internet, in interviews given by your competitors, and especially by asking your customers) that these factors are:

- The number of years in the market
- The degree of notoriety
- The delivery deadlines
- The area of the sales network
- The Sales efficiency per agent
- Post-sale service
- Supplier dependency

And now...

***Where do you find yourself, in relation to the competition?***

Here's a simple but useful tool to determine this: You place the fields above in a diagram with polar positions (big/high to small/little). The diagram will include an assessment of your competitor, compared to the analysis of your company, as follows:

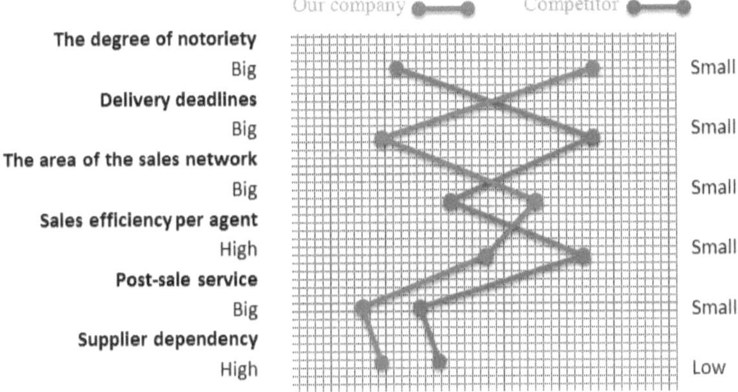


This evaluation is based on the scores assigned both by you AND by the informed persons inside the company. The graph should be repeated for all competitors that the company wants to compare to.

This analysis has diagnostic value and ignites action. Based on the profiles, we can identify discrepancies between our company and the competition, which, if necessary, will have to reduce or broaden them to increase our competitive advantage, **before the crisis** strikes.

And, logically, the next  queation is...

*What small steps are you going to take to improve your business' performance?*

Firstly, there are some features you cannot improve (such as seniority).

Secondly, some features are of no interest. For example: "Our delivery times are better than our competition, and so far, they should not be improved."

For each feature that you need to improve, write the necessary steps. For example:

| Specific Feature | Measurabe Goals |
|---|---|
| Number of years in the market | I'm initiating tasting campaigns and samples campaigns. |
| The degree of notoriety | I increase the sales points in each region by 20%, and I increase the sales on each point by 10%. |
| Delivery deadlines | I set exactly the same sales and the same bonus system as the competition. That way, the sales increase at each point by 10%, which will also lead to the profit being maintained. |
| The area of the sales network | I outsource the service, which generates unjustified costs (such as rare repairs, which keep my employees occupied) to the company specializing in service. |
| Sales efficiency per agent | I only keep suppliers who deliver accurately and on time. In other words, I produce some components, and transform the workshop. |

Don't forget this quote:

***"If you have built castles in the air, your work need not be lost; that is where they should be. Now put the foundations under them."***

Henry David Thoreau

While you're laying your foundations, keep this point in mind...

# 7 Do NOT confuse the key points with the strategy!

Let me tell you a secret: the key factors of success for a company—both during normal times and crises—are roughly the same for all firms in a specific field. They're basically the same for all transportation companies, all metalworking companies, all distribution companies, all training companies, and all medical clinics.

But the factors are different, depending on the field. For instance, they're different for transportation companies and metalworking companies. And the strategies of each company are really different.

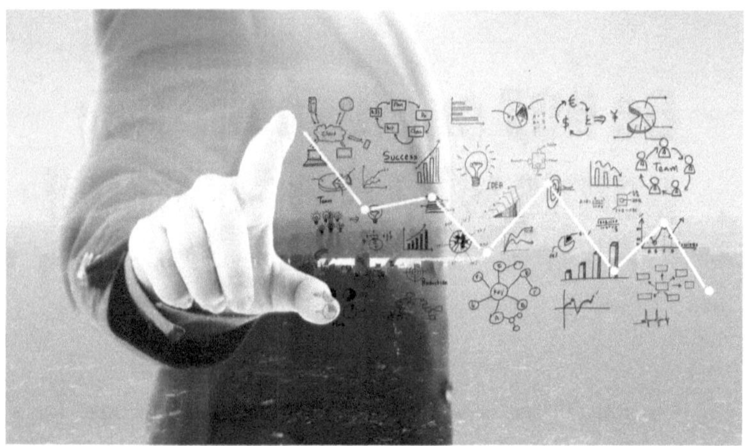

# RECOMMENDATION:

Identify your firm`s key success factors, and see how to extend your firm to reach its highest level (if it should touch it). Then outline your strategy, which you will change when times become troubled. But you have to be the one to change it!

Speaking of strategies...

# 8 Restructure your company before the next crisis begins

The riskiest time to restructure a company is during a full crisis. In times of crisis, your main goal should be stabilization, so you should wait to do any restructuring until after the crisis is over. But the ideal scenario involves restructuring your company **during good times** (like the current climate), not after the storm hits.

In times of crisis, the most important part of strategic planning is the product. So the product itself is important than the pricing. Of course, trying to sell a high-quality product at a high price can prevent purchasing. But trying to sell a low-quality product at a low price won't be profitable either, and it won't result in saving the product from extinction. In addition, during a crisis, you shouldn't withdraw older products from the market, simply because you launched a new product. Old products have covered their costs, and can be sold at lower prices. So they give consumers more choices, and therefore more shopping satisfaction.

Companies wishing to improve their financial performance—as well as companies that want to restructure their activities before the next crisis—use the Ansoff Matrix, which very clearly presents the primary options that they can utilize. Then you can combine the features of your products or services with ways to sell them to the market:

| Product Market | Same product | New product |
|---|---|---|
| Same market | | |
| New market | | |

So it results in these key actions:

- Increasing sales in your market.
- Developing new products for current markets.

- Finding new markets for your current products and services.
- Creating new products for new markets.

The Ansoff Matrix was invented by Russian American Igor Ansoff. It's simple and very effective because it provides a wide range of strategies for growth, and it isn't difficult to use. However, it doesn't factor in the nuances and novelties of the products and markets. A more all-encompassing wider matrix of the relationship between the product and market has been offered by other specialists.[2]

---

**2** M. McDonald, M. Meldrum, *The Complete Marketer*, Kogan Page Publishing House, London, 2013, pag. 176.

| Market | Product novelty | | | | |
|---|---|---|---|---|---|
| | Product / Market | Same product | Extended product | Modified or improved product | New product |
| | Same market | | | | |
| | Greater market coverage | | | | |
| | New coverage, but in related areas | | | | |
| | New market | | | | |

**When applying this matrix, don't forget about this must-don't...**

# 9 Don't diversify your activities before a crisis. Reduce them!

Is it good or bad to diversify your business directions? In times of crisis, the diversification of a product portfolio is a very high temptation.

Here's the reasoning, which I've encountered in many clients: I have to cut prices on current products. When I lower profits, I have to do something to get more revenue.

However, here are two mistakes:

**1.** Looking at incomes, instead of profits. Some believe that more income equals more profits, which is false, especially during a crisis!

2. Forgetting that any diversification of the range results in the first expenditure (which is the hidden spending we've discussed), and involves entering a new territory—where competitors do not sleep, and the risks are uncontrollable.

The more uncontrollable the competitors want to keep a market, the more they narrow it down by doing anything (legal or illegal, moral or immoral) to unlock doors and devour the new visitors.

One of the errors, called "The Waterloo Strategy" by the authors, involves the simultaneous opening of too many fronts. Especially during turbulence, the dispersal of resources can be a fatal move. Another error is "Something for Everyone." More precisely, it's the company's tendency to create a strategy that attracts all kinds of consumers, rather than position themselves in one direction.

The problem with this strategy is the enormous difficulty of finding the right idea that will save your business.

**Before the crisis, I believe that you should:**

- **Diversify your investments.**

I often say, "A table can only stand on four legs." Sometimes people contradict me: "Some tables can stand on three legs." That's true, but no fewer than three legs. It's the same with your business. Although I am not an investment specialist, I try to invest my money in real estate, gold, or silver, rather than stocks and bonds. (I suspect that the latter markets will soon fall.)

- ***Invest* in (don`t start, but invest your money/knowledge in) complementary businesses (or in businesses that will thrive during the next crisis).**

I'm doing this myself, by giving consultancy to a recycling company. We discussed some domains that will thrive **during the next crisis**, and you can find other domains. Rather than diversifying your business in such domains, and blocking your money without being sure that you'll succeed, I advise you to invest in businesses that demonstrate healthy growth, especially those that thrived during the 2008 crisis.

- **Sell new products or services, but only ones that are closely related to your base business.**

Do you currently distribute refreshments? Ok, diversify and sell beer. But no board games!

So, apply the Ansoff Matrix only for the selected areas:

| Market Novelty | Product novelty | | | | |
|---|---|---|---|---|---|
| | Product Market | Same product | Extended product | Modified or improved product | New product |
| | Same market | YES | YES | YES | Not **before the crisis** |
| | Greater market coverage | YES | YES | YES | Not **before the crisis** |
| | New coverage, but in related areas | YES | YES | YES | Not **before the crisis** |
| | New market | YES | YES | YES | Not **before the crisis** |

- **Diversify your territory.**

For example, increase sales outlets, possibly through partnerships with other distributors.

The last secret deserves its own must-do. So if you expand...

# Expand geographically (if possible)

Internet marketing can take you anywhere, especially if you can create something very original, by preparing for customers' needs during the crisis. Find the answer to this question, and you'll be rich:

**"What can I GIVE to increase the HAPPINESS of my existing and future customers?"**

It's fundamental. In another must-do , we'll talk about the secret of keeping customers happy. But first, let me tell you another secret: the winners in the next crisis will concentrate—NOW more than ever—on offering value to customers by sharing their **TALENTS** with an **INCREASING** number of people. They propagate **TALENT** on a **HUGE SCALE**. Why on a "huge scale?" Because even during ordinary times—but especially when a crisis approaches—these components are essential for the survival of your business.

Let's suppose you spend some time teaching a self-defense course (this is one of the business fields we established that will be successful during the next financial crisis, remember?)

Then you can put the course on video, and sell it worldwide. The lessons are applicable, both locally and globally. So why wouldn't you propagate **TALENT** on a **HUGE SCALE**?

In the event of a financial crisis, the e-commerce will continue to develop. That's true, during catastrophes (including the destruction of power sources or cyber-attacks), the electric company will collapse. But it's less probable that this will last too long. After some time, things (including electricity) will probably be relatively normal again. Put aside the need of every business to extend and find partners, and you will have an image of the opportunity of e-commerce when situations stabilize.

So if you want to diversify, expand geographically through e-commerce. That's exactly how I reached you, from a country on the edge of Europe! It requires you to think and act NOW, along with the team, consultants, customers. Yes, but the results have one name: pure prosperity!

So instead of diversifying your products or services, and growing expenses at any price, I advise the contrary, **before the crisis** strikes.

While you're simplifying, keep this must-do in mind...

# 11 Do anything to conserve your business core

Allow me to discuss a metaphor that matches our way of thinking now, before the next crisis...

Isaiah Berlin, a famous social and political theorist, philosopher, and historian of ideas, begins one of his essays on Tolstoy's *Thinking of History* by quoting a passage about the few fragments left behind by the ancient poet Archiloh (680- 645 BC): "The fox knows many things, but the hedgehog knows one big thing." The meaning of this quote is that the fox is able to develop many tricks to grab the prey, while the hedgehog only knows a specific way of defending itself.

Berlin distinguishes between two categories:

- On one hand, there are those who move in different directions. They invest on different levels, hunt in multiple categories, are ready to experience much, think and live without a moral center, and are scatterbrained (like the fox). For them, the world is so varied that it cannot be summed up in a single principle.

- On the other hand, there are those who are guided by a coherent worldview, and practice the guiding principle that always aims at what's important (like the hedgehog). For them, the world contains lots of details, all of which are articulated to create a great principle.

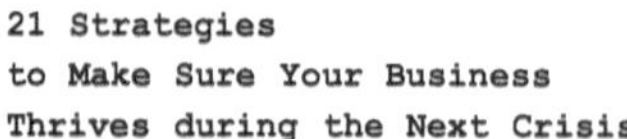



However, neither of the categories can be considered inferior to the others, which means that being a a fox or a hedgehog is only relevant in cases when the strategic resources of the person are required.

The difference between the fox and the hedgehog can be seen by the naked eye anytime, but it really only becomes relevant when two animals are confronted by each other. In these cases, many people would say that it is better to be a hedgehog, since it is sufficient to only know one thing and be successful.

This is a lesson I apply when preparing for the next crisis: do anything to conserve your business core, or the one in the fields that will thrive **during the next crisis**! (See above...)

And as I said when discussing diversification, one of the biggest mistake is to look at incomes, instead of profits. Some believe that more income equals more profits, which is false, especially during a crisis!

**Speaking of profit...**

12

# Always keep in mind the Profit Equation, not the Revenue Equation!

The equation is simple:

**Profit = Income - Costs**

The equation is simple, but a lot of businesspeople do not see the consequences. And if you want your business to survive—or even thrive—**during the next crisis**, now is the time for you to properly understand the meaning of this simple equation.

Let's do a little economic theory, and you'll see how much it will help you before and **during the next crisis**. Your company revenue is formed from the price of the product, and multiplied by the quantity of products sold. The costs are divided into:

- Fixed costs (capital costs, production means, buildings, and land). For example, you pay the same rent for 100 square meters, whether you have 20 employees or 5 employees.

- Variable costs (costs per unit, multiplied by quantity produced, wage costs, materials costs, raw materials, and energy)

Here, I advise my clients to avoid as many fixed costs as possible (such as salaries), and work at variable costs (such as commissions from sales). And I advise you to do the same, when preparing for the next crisis!

To calculate the profit, we must introduce all the components of the income and costs into the equation. Let's take an example of a very simplified calculation.

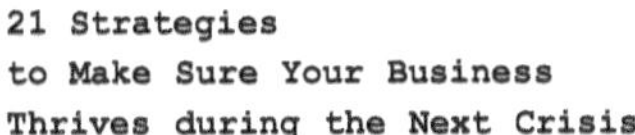

We assume that a company produces 1,500 pens and 600 pencils (quantity) per week, and sells products with 2 euros a piece (price). It gains 600 euro/week.

The rent for the factory is 900 €/week (fixed cost). The staff salary is 1 euro per pen/pencil, and the cost for materials is 0.5 euros per product (variable costs).

```
Revenue = € 2 x 1500 + € 2 x 600 = €4,200
Costs = (1500 + 600) x (1 € + 0,50 €) + 500 €
= 3,650 €
Profit = 4,200 - 3,650 = 550 €
```

**So the company works on profit, doesn't it?**

You can find out by using this table:

| **Products** | | | |
|---|---|---|---|
| | Pens | Pencils | TOTAL |
| Sales (€) | 3,000 | 1,200 | 4,200 |
| **Variable Costs** | | | |
| Materials | 600 | 400 | 1 000 |
| Wages | 800 | 600 | 1 400 |
| Transport | 400 | 400 | 800 |
| TOTAL | 1,800 | 1,400 | 3,20 0 |
| Difference in receipts (€) | 1,200 | -200 | 1 000 |
| Difference in percentages | 40% | -40°/o | |
| **Fixed Costs** | | | |
| Rent | | | 900 |
| Amortization | | | 400 |
| Profit | | | -300 |

The company doesn't make a profit; it records losses. Why? Because of the fixed costs. You can see the contribution that the two products bring to the fixed costs of the company.

That's why I advise my clients to avoid as many fixed costs as possible (such as salaries) and work at variable costs (such as projects or commission from sales and production). Many have started to restructure their company: some employees started working from home, and making an income as a result. The business owner has reduced the space for the company (which means he pays for electricity and heating), and reduced the need for cars. And as I said, the employees were strictly paid for the results. Suddenly, their companies started to work more effectively!

**My advice: perform this analysis for each product, and for each activity area.**

Very near to that is...

# 13 Pay GREAT attention to discounts you offer!

In crisis, a huge temptation for entrepreneurs is to reduce prices. The effect is that it erodes the cash at the disposal of the business. Sometimes, we don't even realize we're selling below the real price, because we're forgetting the fixed costs that we've discussed in this eBook.

Yes, every one of your customers loves (love???) a discount. Entrepreneurs who offer goods and services often use this tactic, even if they do not like it.

But are you perfectly aware of what it means to apply a discount to your earnings?

A retailer buys a box of six wine bottles with 16 euros, and sells it for 20 euros. The retailer's gain is:

20 € - 16 € = 4 €, respectively, **which is a gain of 25% (4/16).**

In terms of a 10% discount on a sale, the winnings change as follows:

€18-€16 = €2, respectively, **which is a gain of 12.5% (2/16).**

**So at a 10% discount, the gain is reduced by 50% [(4-2) / 4 = 0.50)].**

**And then what do we do when a crisis occurs?** Try to sell and preserve profits, in ways other than discounts! And the best way is to:

- Make customers happy
- Bring customers exactly what they want, without loading us with hard-to-sell stocks.

**So we have arrived at a MUST-do before the crisis...**

14

# Attract Customers *Now* Who Will Remain Loyal *during a Crisis*

Have you ever wondered how you can convince customers to buy from YOU and beg YOU to take their money—before and **during the next crisis**? Let me share my experience...

After speaking at a conference, a young guy approached me and started describing his new business idea. He was very enthusiastic! I listened to him for a few minutes, and his ideas were remarkable.

Then I said: "Tell me, why do you intend to start that kind of business?" He stared at me and replied, as if answering an idiot: "Because I need to make money, why else?"

In many cases, the motivation for starting a business is fueled by factors outside the business: "C'mon, honey, let's start a business. We can't go on like this. My friend has a business, and he does very well for himself. Don't you want a SUV and a trip to the Caribbean? We need money, so let's start our business, and collect money from our customers!"

Let's admit it: subconsciously or consciously, many of us use this train of thought. For some time, I thought the same way. However, I realized that this road leads to disaster.

***In the first two years, such thinking destroys 85 out of every 100 businesses. And in the following two to three years, it destroys 13 of the remaining 15 percent.*** These are clear statistics! Only two firms/companies/businesses out of 100 are successful after five years. The rest waste their owner's money, rather than bringing money in and creating prosperity. They go bankrupt. Why?

**Henry Ford,** the famous American car manufacturer (1863-1947), provided an answer: "A business that makes nothing but money is a poor business. A business absolutely devoted to service will have only one worry about profits: they will be embarrassingly large."

Generally, the things that make us happy are safety, comfort, and appreciation. Konosuke Matsushita (the founder of Matsushita Electric) stated, *"Our duty as industrialists is to produce goods for the public, and to enrich and make happier all those who use them. A decrease in profit or a loss of revenue is proof that we have not fulfilled our obligations to society."*

Your business will only expand **IN A HEALTHY WAY** if you:

- Appreciate your customers.
- Take care of them as you would take care of yourself.
- Provide things that make them happy.

Otherwise, you will waste your money, and you will always be in a fog.

While I was preparing our present meeting, I had a discussion with my wife. She has a dentistry practice in a number of villages. For a lot of years, she kept thinking that patients wanted the best-quality materials, and the best technical maneuvers. And that whole time, I told her that her college had taught her this way of thinking, and it's wrong.

Yes, patients need good materials for their fillings and dentures. But they don't care about best-quality materials, and best technical maneuvers. They care about two things:

- The durability of the products
- Not feeling pain. (In Europe, dentists use local anesthetics, not general anesthetics, which they frequently use in the US.)

Because of the raising costs of the dentistry materials she has to use, she wondered: if she raised her prices by 6-10%, wouldn't she lose some of the present customers? I told her that our analysis should start from another point, not from prices.

Her patients really trust her. Why? Although she wants money, she prefers to advise her patients about treatments that are more appropriate for them, even if means that my wife will earn less money.

So her patients return to her, not other dentists. That's why I told her that she must have no fear about raising her prices a little. It's not about prices. People are more concerned about getting good care than low prices. With this understanding, my wife's business will be prepared and successful during the next crises. It also helps that her competition ignores such things. If YOUR competition ignores such things, who do you think will win: you or them?

Because of the care they demonstrate, many businesses will still have loyal customers **during the next crisis**, EVEN IF THEY HAVE HIGHER PRICES THAN THEIR COMPETITORS. Even with lower prices, their monthly profits are lower because they treat their customers carelessly. Or they even treat them with condescension and disdain, as if they're pigs who are only good for providing bacon.

Consider the way Walt Disney succeeded at creating animated films. Even after his death, his studios make successful movies. Why? Because he wrote the guideline that his successors are still following, which is NOT profit-centered but CLIENT-centered: *"The inclination of my life has been to do things and make things which will give pleasure to people in new and amazing ways. By doing that, I please and satisfy myself."*

*Was Walt Disney a winner? Definitely, yes!* Moreover, Disney continuously rebrands itself, which is why it continues to win.

It is the product or service that pays, not the employer. Care toward customers, not your profit plan, ensures success. Therefore, here is the secret **that is within your reach, as of today**. Customer satisfaction is no longer enough. Today, you need customers who are delighted, not merely content.

Previously, it was sufficient for a cab driver to transport you safely to your destination. Then things evolved. Cab drivers were expected to drive smoothly, so the passenger won't get sick in the car. And depending on the situation, they're expected to either carry on a conversation or remain silent (if you're not in the mood to talk).

But these innovations are **NO LONGER** enough. Today, taxi companies win customers by making them happy—primarily through two things:
After you place the order, they arrive quickly.
The driver helps you with your luggage, possibly carrying it to your hotel, house, or apartment.

Merely getting you somewhere was satisfying decades ago, but customers now have other requirements, such as quick arrival, conversation, a comfortable climate in the car, and good customer service. You keep returning to the same cab company because they meet your needs. So you want to travel **with them**, and you will remain loyal **to them** during a crisis

***So say NO to this mentality: "Let's take their money, so we can afford a vacation in the Caribbean." No one succeeds like that, yet 85% of new entrepreneurs think in this manner (either consciously or subconsciously), and fail. The Fundamental Secret to preparing your business for the upcoming crisis and to* attracting customers NOW who will remain loyal d*uring a crisis is...***

Switch from satisfying **your** needs to meeting your **client's** needs. Then customers will beg YOU to take their money now—and in the future—regardless of hyperinflation, and whether or not they have money. They will specifically beg YOU, not your competitors! Small and large companies survive crises by learning this secret.

Here's a second MUST-do...

# 15 Bring customers exactly what they want

Some will say, “Yeah, that’s an old model.” That’s right! How many of us use it?

Before a crisis, it’s no longer sufficient to "bring customers exactly what they want"—if you want loyal customers **during the next crisis**!

What can you do? In order for you to thrive and prepare for the next crises, WRITE this down NOW: "What can I GIVE to increase the HAPPINESS of my existing and future customers?"

It’s the fundamental Secret.

Write it on your desktop. Write it on your bathroom mirror. Write it in the halls. Make anything to permanently see it. And apply it!

To clarify, I said "give," not "sell." Now write it a few more times, and put it on your desk, pin it on the wall, and tape it on your bathroom mirror.

The hairdresser, the architect, the mechanic, the IT specialist, and the consultant all earn thousands of Euros per month. First, they give. What do they give? Some would say, "Advice." Wrong! They give **the certainty of the right decision.** (If you do not believe this concept, try cutting your hair yourself!) Of course, in order to get repeat business, they have to give a good haircut, correct?

But the businesspeople that will survive—even thrive—in the next crises offer more than mere products or services: they offer **genuine care** to their customers—starting now!

Keep in mind that the most common desire in the entire world is happiness. Allow me to explain something: when I refer to "happiness," I do not only mean "joy." I mean anything that increases the value and the performance or competitiveness of your customer, and makes them happy. Everything that brings appropriate solutions to their problems makes them happy. Anything that improves their wealth, health, or physical appearance will make them happy. Also, anything that gives your customers more power or intelligence makes them happy.

Why do you think I insisted on listing the fields that will thrive during a crisis? Now you have the answer: because these fields make people HAPPY. Anything that you can give people what they need now—and when a crisis occurs—will make them happy. Then they will be YOUR customers, and no one else's. You will receive their money, not your competitors. Sounds great, right?

Generally, the things that make us happy are safety, comfort, and appreciation. Konosuke Matsushita (the founder of Matsushita Electric) stated, *"Our duty as industrialists is to produce goods for the public,and to enrich and make happier all those who use them. A decrease in profit or a loss of revenue is proof that we have not fulfilled our obligations to society."*

**How can you make your customers ask YOU to take their money?** Do you wish to know the secret? I'll bet you do! Regardless of whether you're selling agricultural products, consultancy, or courses, you must satisfy at least one of the above desires. Only then will you become rich from your business.

How can you provide safety, care, and happiness when selling bread? Imagine entering a shop that carries inexpensive, regular-quality bread, but smells quite neglected. You receive a loaf of bread from the shopkeeper. He has just wiped his child's runny nose with his bare hands, then immediately handles the bread that he gives you. The shopkeeper absentmindedly counts the change, then turns his back on you the next second, even though you want to buy something else.

Then imagine a brilliantly clean shop, which carries several types of bread. The seller asks, "Which kind would you like? White, dark, semi-white, sliced, or unsliced?" Then the seller informs you that she has just received some delicious pastries—the ones she knows you're crazy about. And tomorrow, she will receive some fantastic cakes, all of which spare you from running around that evening when your guests arrive.

Which shop will you go back to, and purchase sodas, fruit, water, cakes, wine, and liquor for your guests tomorrow? Which store will you **insist** on taking YOUR money? The store with the cheap bread, or the one with slightly more expensive goods? You will shop at the second store many times, and you will spend hundreds of dollars there because the shopkeeper was kind and attentive when you bought a loaf of bread.

You will fill the wallet of the one who:

- Took CARE of you
- Showed you APPRECIATION
- Created COMFORT for you
- Provided CERTAINTY that you made the best choice when you purchased a small item

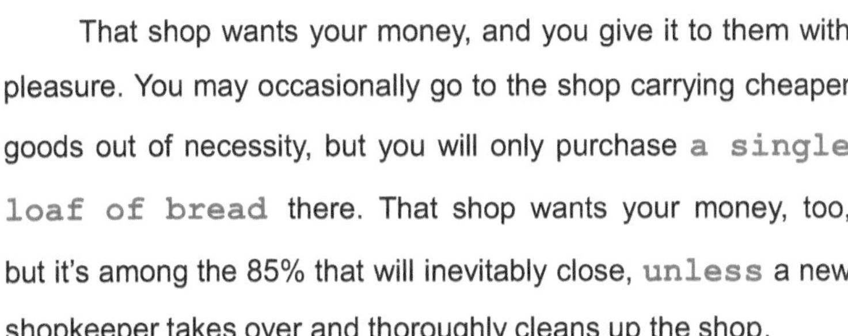

That shop wants your money, and you give it to them with pleasure. You may occasionally go to the shop carrying cheaper goods out of necessity, but you will only purchase a single loaf of bread there. That shop wants your money, too, but it's among the 85% that will inevitably close, unless a new shopkeeper takes over and thoroughly cleans up the shop.

*So remember to WRITE this down and post it everywhere: "What can I GIVE to increase the HAPPINESS of my existing and future customers?"*

"Bring customers exactly what they want." Is it an old model? Yes, it is. Renew it, by making customers happy. **During the next crisis**, such a strategy is crucial, and you need to start it (you guessed it) NOW!

Having stated these Secrets, the time has arrived to shift perspectives. As I said, there's no other way. So I urge you to think about what have YOU have done to ensure that YOUR company satisfies customers at the highest level, delights them, makes them happy, and takes care of them.

For instance, do you have a construction company? If so, are your customers looking for an architect? Recommend one, even if you must make several telephone calls. **Help your customer**. Make customers happy. **Then in times of crisis, happy customers will save your business.**

But don't stop there. There's one more crucial MUST-do, which makes the difference between touching and missing your objectives.

Inform all of your departments about the results of this survey, and ensure that they know **exactly** what they must do. Ford said something else that I often tell companies, and that I often repeat when I provide training or business consultancy: *"It is not the employer who pays the wages. Employers only handle the money. It is the **customer** who pays the wages."*

You start by making sure that your employees and collaborators show your customers the attention and responsiveness that they prefer.

**And speaking of employees...**

# 16 Only retain people who are willing to be flexible, adaptable, and make customers happy!

In one way or another, many have said that real entrepreneurs do not build businesses. Rather, entrepreneurs build teams that build businesses. Why? Because I can do better than you think you can, or you don't know how to do better. The secret is to find the team that will devote their efforts in this direction, much more now than in the past.

Mark Zuckerberg recognized this concept. In fact, he said, *"The most important thing for you as an entrepreneur trying to build something is: you need to build a really good team. And that's what I spend all my time on."*

Why? Because Zuckerberg also anticipates the crisis that will happen. And now, **before the crisis**, it is NOT important to develop the business. Instead, it's important to develop a team that will succeed during times of uncertainty, when many will fail.

Well, everything is changing now, **before the crisis**, as we have just seen above. Do you know how it will go? Probably not. And you don't know NOW what you will sell during the crisis, do you?

Realize that you do not know how you're going to lead your business. We previously discussed which businesses will survive during the crisis. Is your business among those mentioned? Do you know what you will sell during the crisis? What conclusion will you reach if you currently distribute coffee machines or shoes? What if the solution is that you should distribute wheat or self-defense gear?

Yes! That's it! Your company must become flexible! And for your business to become flexible, the first law is that **your people** must be flexible.

I recall a client who hired a human resources employee for sixty employees. Now let's be honest: after having completed sixty labor contracts, internal HR documents, and other related documents, that person didn't have very much work to do. My client was a manufacturer of very beautiful, plated glassware. When I arrived at his company one day, I saw the HR employee sticking colored labels onto crystal cups destined for export. This situation really amazed me, because the economy was normal. Somewhat ironically, I asked the lady, "Is this part of your HR job description?" She looked at me and said, "To earn a living, I must do this also."

Keep this in mind (or better yet, ingrain it into the minds of your team): to prepare for the crisis, you must be flexible to earn a living! So **only** retain people who are willing to do more than what's written in their job descriptions. During crises, you must be flexible, as Noah and his sons were, or you will die!

What must you do to succeed? Combine duties! You must seriously think about what you want.

It's your choice: as a trial, you can give your accountant a few simple contracts at the beginning. If your mechanic only does actual work during 75% of his shift, it's up to you to assign delivery and driving duties to him. If the secretary doesn't have much work to do, it's up to you to train her to input basic data from the primary accounting. And it's up to you to have the customer-support manager assist the design team.

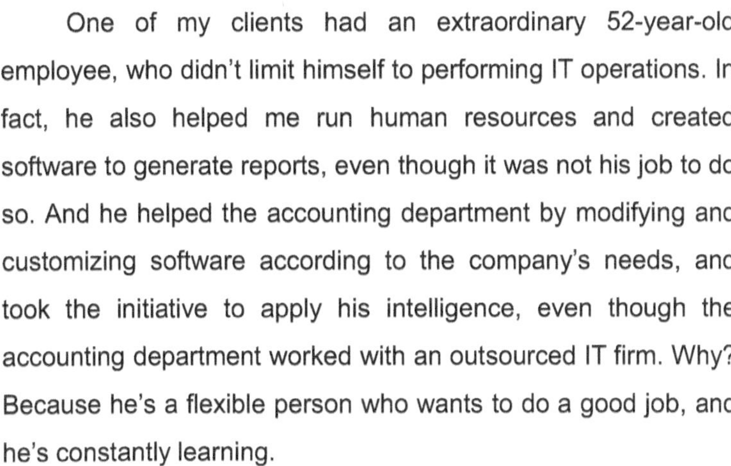

One of my clients had an extraordinary 52-year-old employee, who didn't limit himself to performing IT operations. In fact, he also helped me run human resources and created software to generate reports, even though it was not his job to do so. And he helped the accounting department by modifying and customizing software according to the company's needs, and took the initiative to apply his intelligence, even though the accounting department worked with an outsourced IT firm. Why? Because he's a flexible person who wants to do a good job, and he's constantly learning.

If you prepare for the next crisis by training your employees, you could prevent one of your departments from being dissolved, or one of your employees from being let go. That way, you will always have a team by your side that is prepared to take over some of the duties of other departments or colleagues.

**Do you want more? If so, why not do the next step?**

# 17 Put your team on autopilot now, before the next crisis strikes

In my activity as a consultant, when improving my clients' business, I often started from a very clear reality, which I viewed as being the reverse of the traditional point of view. My performance appraisal (PA) system provides the connection between the rewards that employees hope to receive and the productivity they achieve.

Here's the proper sequence: `Productivity leads to a good appraisal, which leads to a reward`. This sequence is logical, but the reverse of it is not!

However, employees generally see things in the exact opposite order, and many managers do not know how to implement the correct order.

Remember, there is *no solution* other than this sequence:

**Productivity ⇒ PA ⇒ Reward**

If one of these items is missing or is incorrectly defined, then employees no longer receive the rewards they deserve.

Do you want to make your team work on autopilot now, **before the crisis** strikes? Link the performance that the company needs to the motivation that employees need. And if you didn't do it properly before, it's time to implement it now, **before the crisis** strikes.

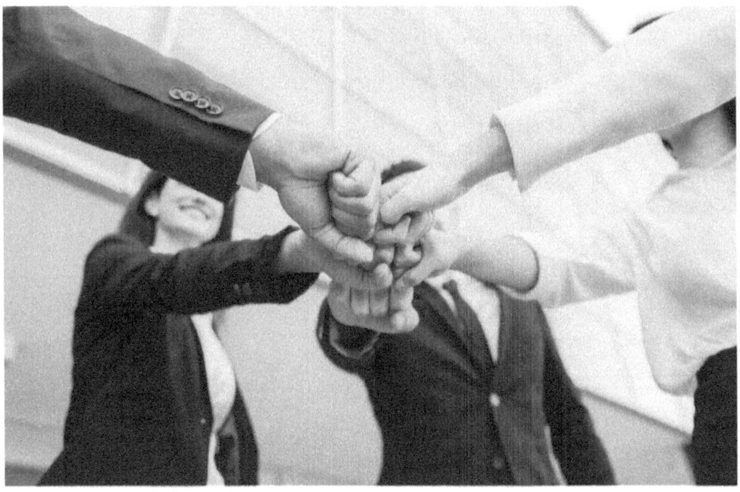

In a sale, the formula is simple: you give me a car, and I give you the money for the car. And ultimately, a PA system is equally simple: you give me the performance standards, the flexibility, and the discipline I need, and I'll give you the salary you need. (In fact, I will give anyone a raise who can increases his/her performance to this level.)

I initiated a PA system at a transportation company in 2009 (when we were in full crisis mode). Within 3 years, it gained the first prize for Central and Eastern Europe. This company's testimonial is featured on my blog.

I don't know of any other, better system for increasing the value of employees' qualifications than full appraisals of the performance, skills, and knowledge of each employee. Only then can you discover the optimal way to use its capacities. For this reason, a PA system is another key to success **during the next crisis**.

By evaluating now, **before the crisis**, you will get your employees **used to these procedures and criteria**, so they will accept that their wages will be linked to their performances during the crisis. They will **not** be based on mere seniority, and **not** on the criteria they think—but on the standards and criteria that your company maintains.

I urge you to make these preparations before the next crisis, so your people have time to accommodate them when times are still peaceful. The procedures relieve stress for you and your employees, so implement them now, during peaceful times, rather than applying them when you and your employees are already under stress.

**Here is the simple answer to this question: why should I start now, before the crisis? Because the results will be better, and you'll enter the crisis with your homework done.**

# 18 Reduce your spending and losses

This point is crucial to the success of your business during a crisis. But as always, you have to prepare now, **before the crisis**.

My advice **before the crisis**: beware of the losses you do not feel NOW!

The fact that machines are often damaged is a "tearless injury" for many entrepreneurs. They are the equivalent of equipment failure, and result in a decrease in revenue. In fact, machine failure leads to expenses that few entrepreneurs have quantified: it takes time and money to put people into operation. The defective parts and the materials used for the repair tests also cost less. Lower-performance machines require less hours and manpower, even when working with lower efficiency or waiting for machine repair.

Therefore, in order to become more profitable now, **before the crisis**, reduce both the visible costs (for example, stocks that are very hard to sell) and the "invisible" ones, by answering the following questions:

- How much does an hour of interruption or inefficient use cost? Your accountant can help you make a calculation!
- What steps do you take to reduce unnecessary hours for various reasons?
- Is the production well-coordinated with the distribution? Do the sales agents have the same rhythm with production, and vice versa? If not, you may lose customers because of your lack of coordination between production and sales. Or on the contrary, you may be overloaded with stocks of raw materials or finished products, which also generates expenses.
- What do you do to make your employees more flexible? How do you offset periods in which more effort is needed with periods with less effort—without incurring additional costs?

Is it hard to reduce unjustified losses and costs? Certainly, yes! Now, when it's peaceful, it's difficult for you to reduce these unjustified losses and expenses, correct? So how hard will it be to reduce these expenses when the crisis crashes your last bit of energy? Do you think you'll have time for that kind of adjustment?

If you start moving these subtle mechanisms that your money flows through NOW, you will thrive during a crisis. But by far, the best way to reduce spending and losses is to eliminate the overuse of resources. In order to achieve this goal, the following seven activities must be simultaneously carried out:

- Improving quality
- Improving productivity
- Reducing stocks
- Shortening the production line
- Reducing machine drops
- Reducing space
- Reducing delivery time

Eliminating these woes will lead to a reduction in the overall cost of operations.

**Beware: I said: "simultaneously". Why do you think I used that word?**

19

# Only develop partnerships that will utilize economic recessions as opportunities

Partnerships involve the economic concept of sharing resources. In other words, it's best to combine everyone's resources and share them, in order to reduce costs and increase the accessibility of products and services. This tactic can bring about growth with fewer resources, and without tying up money in equipment, facilities, or people. And you won't block money from flowing. Likewise, penetrating new markets via alliances or partnerships is the ideal approach during pre-crisis times.

To emphasize: in a partnership, 1 + 1 + 1 = 8. Within strategic partnerships, possibilities are great—both in "normal" times and when preparing for a crisis. Partnerships can generate money and fill many people's pockets, yet few people form them. Remember, partnerships are crucial when preparing for a crisis.

Of course, you have to avoid many problems when preparing your business for a future crisis. Of all the sources of failure in partnerships that I have experienced and read about, I've found that you can find the best synthesis here.

If you avoid the ones written there, create a plan to harness the ADVANTAGES, and eliminate the SOURCES OF ERROR, you have taken another step toward a prosperous business during times of crisis.

**And now here's the best part about the promise I made earlier:** **s**trategic partnerships tend to multiply quickly. ***And so does money.*** If you can associate your brand with three or four partners that you have carefully chosen, you can develop momentum and attract even more.

But beware! Strategic partnership is NOT something you can treat randomly. It's not something you can just "do when you have time." If you **expect** to have good time, it will never come. On the contrary, it is an essential component of your monthly and quarterly planning process NOW, **before the crisis**.

If you use partnerships, the crisis means double or triple revenues to you! But *only if* you prepare in advance.

**Remember this:** Dare. Don't ever say that you're too small!

Start knocking on the doors of the big partners, so you'll already be in their minds when a crisis occur. Only keep flexible employees who do good jobs. Analyze which business costs don't add any value, and give them up. Revise the contracts, so they can help you.

## By the way...

# Prepare contracts that will protect you during hard times

In crises, contracts must have special clauses to protect you. Then the question arises: Can people without a legal education make a contract to protect them?

I say yes. What exactly do you need? The key is related to forecasting possible scenarios: what happens if a client does not receive the goods you sent him, if he does not pay, or if he only makes a partial payment? What happens if you don't give him what he wants (and you say it's exactly what he asked you to do)? What happens if you cannot hand over the merchandise, or if the merchandise is inconsistent? What are the penalties for nonexecution or cancellation of the contract?

Write out your asnswers to these questions. Here's a secret: I always think of a possible litigation. Times may become troubled, so you need assurance in writing. Don't worry about what your partner will think. A solid contract is a sign of strength and firmness on your part. Therefore, he'll see you as a trusted partner, regardless of the way the documents are written. A strong person is organized and attentive to the smallest detail. So certain clauses are absolutely necessary.

I have prepared my crisis contracts by inserting the following clauses:

- A renegotiation clause (if I do not like the conditions, but I want to continue the business relationship with that partner)
- An arbitration clause (extremely useful in quickly recovering money, especially in times of hyperinflation)
- Guarantees (letters of credit, escrow, personal guarantees by the owners of the debts), which should answer these questions:
- Under what conditions are notifications accepted between partners (verbal and written)?
- How does the contract terminate?

Is it necessary to discuss these clauses with a professional jurist or lawyer? Most often, it depends on the contract. For some contracts, a simple completion with the above clauses is enough.

As a synthesis of all we've discussed till now, check out the last must-do:

21

# Turn to New Leadership before the crisis

## (which is different from Leadership during normal times)

What would it be like to encounter this situation? Together with your team of employees and collaborators, you make a monthly plan for rescuing your business from the next crisis. In the first month, it works well. But in the second month, the sales component has worse results than you expected. On the first day of the third month, you tell your employees, and you spend all day seeking solutions to compensate for the previous month.

That night, you go home, and you don't get much sleep. The crisis is approaching, and your plan is already failing. Finally, in the early morning, you get some tormented sleep for a few hours. Or you thought you would...

Suddenly, the phone rings. It's 7 in the morning! And someone is calling you from the office! Rattled, you answer, and you hear the voice of one of your employees: "Boss, could you come into the office? We have to tell you something…"

At 7 in the morning? Why are they calling you from the office, when you told them to only call you if something urgent occurred? What could you have possibly missed since the night before?

Still dizzy because you haven't eaten, you get into your car, and drive to your office to break someone's neck. When you get there, all your employees are staring at you. They don't know where to start...

After a while, one brave employee says: "Yesterday, I noticed that you were worried about the results, boss. Look, last night, we all stayed until 9 pm. And this morning, we came in an hour early to find ways to compensate for last month's lack of accomplishments. Do you want us to present our solutions to you?"

How does it feel to live through this kind of experience during a crisis? Does that seem like something you'd want to hear?

It would be great to have this kind of staff, wouldn't it? But where can you find such employees? Well, that's what we're going to discuss now. You actually don't have to find them. Instead, make them find you.

Put your team on autopilot. Motivate your pleople. And get rid of the who don't want to do good work, to be flexible, and to work like a team. If you do not take advantage of opportunities to implement substantial changes before the new crisis, you will be in danger of wasting a fantastic opportunity for efficiency: you need to cut off the dead branches, and only keep the healthy core that will help you reach the shore. If you plan ahead, you can thrive during a tsunami, while others are drowning.

**Before the crisis, leadership will only:**

- Communicate transparently and clearly.
- Practice what they preach.
- Encourage and reward the discovery and exposure of new methods.

This kind of leadership works during normal times. But New Leadership will do ALL of the things listed above, but in a flexible way that will save your business.

You already know the formula for New Leadership, since we discussed it above:

- **Only keep flexible people near you**.

Then you'll be able to learn more about their job postings now than you will when you're sailing the stormy sea. By helping you, these people will also be in a ship that will guarantee that they will keep their careers stay afloat. So train them. Evaluate them by using the simple-but-effective tools that I have provided for you.

- **Be prepared to change the direction of your business.**

We have discussed a few possible directions, but of course, there are many more possible directions. For instance, there will certainly be more opportunities on a regional level.

- **Pay attention to details.**

Facilitate the necessary changes that we discussed, which is a detail that your stressed competitor did not notice could save your business.

- **Make sure your contracts have all the essential clauses.**

Then you will save your business when hard times come. Then your business partners will sign contracts without being suspicious, while the times are still normal. These adjustments will help you a lot **during the next crisis**. Yes, that's one new component of New Leadership.

- **Start cutting costs, but not *at any cost*.**

If you have offered your employees expensive vacations up until now, ask them what they would prefer instead. You may be surprised to see how understanding they are, and how willing they are to give up anything that does not bring value.

Allow me to elaborate on what New Leadership **before the crisis** means...

During the 2008 crisis, the owner of a production company called in a consultant. The owner gave him a tour of the entire company. And with growing astonishment, the consultant noticed that the company was working at full capacity, and wanted to expand during a crisis.

The owner hadn't called the consultant to give him advice about keeping the doors open or avoiding bankruptcy. Rather, he wanted to know how to facilitate growth, because they could no longer handle all the orders!

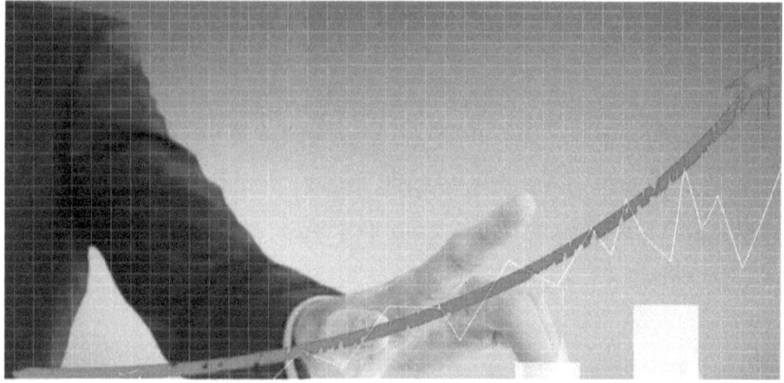

Continuing to be astonished, the consultant asked the owner: *"How did you succeed to this extent, when so many others have gone bankrupt?"*

The owner replied: *"**Before the crisis**, our competitors sought to obtain government support and the best credit. They diversified their businesses in all directions, because all directions were profitable. But the economy was overheated, so all types of merchandise were accepted. Then we changed our minds. Instead of government facilities hiding the lack of performance and efficiency, we fought to improve quality, and to become more efficient **through our own resources**.*

*We haven't touched a bank loan, and we didn't purchase costly technologies. But we have improved our products, and searched for good partners in the market. We only kept people who wanted to be flexible, and to remain near us in both good and bad times.*

*So when the crisis came, our employees were already prepared. We built good relationships with customers and partners, and our quality processes were tested.*

*My competitors were not concerned about these issues, so they hadn't applied for government support (which the country could no longer provide anyway). One after another, they lost sales, or even went bankrupt. We contacted some of their former customers, but a lot of them asked us to take them on. And at this moment, we can't manage all the orders. I urgently need to reorganize my company, in order to successfully honor as many orders as possible—and maintain the same quality. And that's why I called you, Mr. Smithers."*

I want to tell you a secret now, before our time together is over: the size of a company does not relate to whether or not it succeeds. Both large companies and small businesses have succeeded and thrived. Big companies (including Lehman Brothers, Fannie Mae, Merrill Lynch, and Bear Stearns) have gone bankrupt. The number of employees didn't matter during previous crises, and it won't matter during the next one.

In the story above, the company ran at full speed during a crisis, despite being in a poor country. Their secret lied in the fact that they managed to prepare themselves, and they took advantage of their geography to successfully transform their own business.

"The best way to predict the future is to invent it."
Alan Kay, American computer scientist

Yes, that's leadership **before the crisis**: invent your own future.

The answers to your questions about the crisis already exist. Opportunities float in the air, especially during a crisis. Some are visible; others can only be seen when we intersect with them. But they do exist.

# CONCLUSION

I have gathered and shared all the basic information that is absolutely critical for you to make your business grow and prosper **during the next crisis**. So get excited: a new opportunity will come to you! Are you prepared?

The treasure is the same for everyone. The favorable wind blows for all—big and small, young and old, rich and poor.

Do not forget this short poem:

*One ship sails east,*
*And another west,*
*By the self-same winds that blow,*
*Tis the set of the sails*
*And not the gales,*
*That tells the way we go.*

- Ella Wheeler Wilcox

It's your turn now. What do **you** say? Are you one of the leaders in this embryo of a new (and perhaps healthier) economy?

I think you are. Or you may be. In either case, the next step is waiting for the crisis—with motivated and flexible people, good partnerships, the best contract clauses, and loyal clients.

Guess who will thrive and gather the clients from businesses that will go bankrupt?

We will go on...

Life goes on, so will we. What's the biggest challenge you encounter at your business? What problem do you want me to send you solutions to? Explain it in a few words, and send it to me at hello@horatiu.biz. Then my team and I we will find personalized solutions for YOU!

If you need help, let me know. That's what I'm here for!

I prepared my business to thrive **during the next crisis**. I urge you to study this formula, as it will help your business thrive **during the next crisis**. Then try to adapt it to your business.

# ABOUT THE AUTHOR

**Horaţiu Sasu** has dual specialization: legal counselor and economist (marketing and performance in Human Resources Management).

He has advised both private companies and public departments. His 19 years of experience of advising experience have included:

- Increasing the performances of the company and the employees

- Outsourcing the activities and using the collaborators
- Increasing the number of clients
- Increasing the company's profits (in normal times and during crises)
- Personally training employees (with the objective of increasing job performances and profits)
- Creating and implementing HR procedures (such as avoiding labor disputes)

The author currently works as a trainer and business consultant, and is available for a limited number of speaking engagements and consulting assignments. See opinions, solutions, and articles about preparing your business for crises at www.horatiu.biz.

www.ingramcontent.com/pod-product-compliance
Lightning Source LLC
Chambersburg PA
CBHW030947240526
45463CB00016B/2030